TRAVAILING
PRAYER
BIRTHING REVIVAL

MICHAEL MARCEL

UKWELLS.ORG

Published by UK Wells.
Website: www.ukwells.org

Table of Contents

Introduction

In my book 'Prepare for Revival', I list four disciplines/ anointings that, in my opinion, we are lacking in the Body of Christ today:

- Holiness
- Travailing Prayer
- Evangelism
- Testimony

I believe these areas are the main reasons why we have not had a revival in England for nearly one hundred years.

I have taken two of these subjects, Holiness and Travailing Prayer and turned them into booklets because I feel these are vital to our nation. Both booklets point the reader to revival/ evangelism and they are both full of testimonies.

Testimony is really powerful; it brings breakthrough. The word testimony in Hebrew is 'aydooth' which, according to a Hebrew scholar means 'do it again with the same power and authority'. Every time you speak out or read a testimony you are saying to the Lord, 'do it again with the same power and authority'.

I have read several accounts of love-feasts, where Methodist Society members gathered together to worship and give testimonies, that led to revival and cases where revivals have been read out and new revivals have begun. Please remember this as you read these accounts. The language these writers use is not modern English but the stories are still impacting.

My understanding of Travailing Prayer has developed over

the last five years and the more I research the more my understanding continues to grow.

My job as an author is to look at how God moved in the past and to highlight to the Church anything that may have been forgotten over time. My only interest is in revival and in this booklet, how prayer relates to revival. The United Kingdom is in a truly dreadful place and the only answer is a great revival that will bring about a significant reformation of our society.

Travailing Prayer has brought breakthrough into revival on several occasions, but today it is little known about, which is why I have written this booklet. Why has it gone out of fashion? Perhaps the word 'Travail' puts people off. Some friends, in fact, tried to get me to change the title for this reason. I could have called it, Prevailing Prayer, Birthing Prayer or Breakthrough Prayer, but 'travail' is a Biblical word and it describes very well the sort of prayer it is.

Chapter One

Definition and Biblical Context

The English Oxford living dictionary defines the verb 'travail' as:

> "Engage in painful or laborious effort" or "a woman being in labour"

That is a definition that would put anybody off. The best definition I have found for Travailing Prayer is by James Goll, a significant prophetic voice in the USA.

> "Travail is a form of intense intercession given by the Holy Spirit whereby an individual or group is gripped by something that grips God's heart. The individual or group labours with Him for an opening to be created so that the new life can come forth."[1]

A practical example of Travailing Prayer is given by Dutch Sheets, another American prophetic voice and intercessor:

> "I was probably nine or ten years old and it occurred while praying for an unsaved aunt. One night as I lay in bed, I felt a strong burden to pray for her salvation. I remember getting out of my bed, onto my knees and weeping uncontrollably, asking God to save her... probably for thirty minutes or an hour. Finally, the burden lifted and I went to sleep.
>
> My aunt lived about an hour and a half away from

us. For some 'unknown' reason however, she called us later that week and said she wanted to come to our church that Sunday morning. We did not know at the time that she was actually coming to the service planning to give her life to Christ, and did."[2]

The most common association with the word 'Travail' is birthing which is not surprising as when one travails what is happening is that Holy Spirit is using you to birth His plans and purposes. Those plans may be to bring salvation to someone or to many, to bring rain in a drought, to bring healing to the sick etc.

There are many examples of Travailing Prayer in the Bible.

> *"Before she travailed, she brought forth; before her pain came, she was delivered of a man child. Who hath heard such a thing? who hath seen such things? Shall the earth be made to bring forth in one day? or shall a nation be born at once? for as soon as Zion travailed, she brought forth her children."* (Isaiah 66:7-8)

Zion represents Israel, but it also represents the Church, so this is a verse that relates to new believers coming to salvation through Travailing Prayer.

> *"And Elijah said unto Ahab, "Get thee up, eat and drink; for there is a sound of abundance of rain." So Ahab went up to eat and to drink. And Elijah went up to the top of Carmel; and he cast himself down upon the earth, and put his face between his knees, and said to his servant, "Go up now, look toward the sea." And he went up, and looked, and said, "there is nothing." And he said, "Go again" seven times. And it came to pass at the seventh time, that he said, "Behold, there ariseth a little cloud out of the sea, like a man's hand." And he said, "Go up, say unto*

Ahab, "Prepare thy chariot, and get thee down that the rain stop thee not. '" (1 Kings 18:41-44)

Here Elijah is praying in the birthing position and birthed rain. Please note that in verse one of the Chapter the Lord tells Elijah that He is going to send rain. Travailing will always start with the Lord; it is not something we initiate. It might be a word from the Lord telling us what we are travailing for or you may find yourself travailing under the power of Holy Spirit and have no idea why.

In the New Testament:

"Jesus left the upper room with his disciples and, as was his habit, went to the Mount of Olives, his place of secret prayer. There he told the apostles, 'Keep praying for strength to be spared from the severe test of your faith that is about to come.' Then he withdrew from them a short distance to be alone. Kneeling down, he prayed, 'Father, if you are willing, take this cup of agony away from me. But no matter what, your will must be mine.' Jesus called for an angel of glory to strengthen him, and the angel appeared. He prayed even more passionately, like one being sacrificed, until he was in such intense agony of spirit that his sweat became drops of blood, dripping onto the ground." (Luke 22:39-44 TPT)

Through his prayers He achieved victory in the Spirit over the trial that was ahead of Him.

"To this day we are aware of the universal agony and groaning of creation, as if it were in the contractions of labour for childbirth. And it's not just creation. We who have already experienced the first fruits of the Spirit also inwardly groan as we passionately long to experience our full status as God's sons and daughters - including our physical bodies being transformed." (Romans 8:22-3 TPT)

Travailing Prayer will usually be for Intercessors as they are generally open to the Lord using them that way, so that they can pull heaven down to earth. But it can also be for anyone who is willing to be used by Holy Spirit to birth something.

There may be a cost involved; perhaps time because travailing may take as little time as a few minutes or it may take days, depending when the burden lifts; perhaps discomfort, as the pain may vary from nothing, to some tiredness, to the pain a woman experiences in childbirth; or perhaps weeping or groaning as these are common manifestations, and emotions may vary from feeling troubled or depressed to distress.

One may also be woken by God in the middle of the night with a burden to pray for someone who will probably be in some sort of danger, or for a national or local issue.

The power of travailing prayer is clearly vital to the bringing of an awakening. There may also be a need for prayers of repentance regarding the area or the nation.

> *"If at any time I announce that a nation or kingdom is to be uprooted, torn down and destroyed, and if that nation I warned repents of its evil, then I will relent and not inflict on it the disaster I had planned. And if at another time I announce that a nation or kingdom is to be built up and planted, and if it does evil in my sight and does not obey me, then I will reconsider the good I had intended to do for it."* (Jeremiah 18:7-10 NIV)

In the book of Daniel, sometimes his praying was identificational repentance on behalf of his people. I am sure that this is a type of prayer that many will do before a revival, in case the Lord is withholding His blessing because of the sin of the people.

Chapter Two

Travailing Prayer in Revival

A revival may be expected when Christians have a spirit of prayer for a revival. That is, when they pray as if their hearts were set upon it. When Christians have the spirit of prayer for a revival. When they go about groaning out their hearts desire. When they have real travail of soul.

Charles Finney

I should imagine that the first characteristic of a revival that you would think of is prayer. Most of the accounts of major revivals that I have read, trace their history back to one or more people praying for God to move. Pastors sometimes call prayer meetings for revival, hoping that the gathering of people together to ask the Lord to send revival will bring it about.

Inevitably, what I am about to say will be thought of as controversial by some, but I do not believe that the masses praying will bring an awakening. In a way, this statement is obvious, because there has been much prayer on this subject in England over the last 98 years, and yet there is no awakening!

There are two extreme views on what brings revival. At one end of the spectrum we have Charles Finney, that great American revivalist, who believed that if we did actions a, b, c and d, revival would always come. So, basically, God will just react to what we want. I do not believe this is correct. Many people have tried to follow Finney's formula, but nobody, as far as I know, has succeeded.

The other extreme view is that it is all to do with the Sovereignty of God; therefore, it does not matter what we do, God will bring revival whenever He wants. I believe this is wrong as well, as plainly Scripture shows that God wants to work with us, and through us, to bring about His plans and purposes - healing, salvation, etc.

So, having disagreed with the two extremes, I certainly fall closer to the Sovereignty of God than I do to Finney's view. What worked for Finney was either because he was ministering in an atmosphere of revival, or because he was carrying an extraordinary revivalist anointing; often both were present. I believe that God decides when He wants to bring revival, He then tells this to his prophets and intercessors, who in turn begin to declare and pray it in. It is a partnership. Of course, some may not know that they are responding to God's wishes; they may think that the idea came from them, but that is the way I believe it works.

The Lord told Jeremiah that the people of Israel would be in Babylon for seventy years, but He had a better future for them and He would bring them into that future when they prayed for it. Eventually, Daniel studied the past and in doing so recognised the prophetic word. He was the one who prayed (travailed) into being what God had already planned.

> *"For I know the plans I have for you," declares the LORD, "plans to prosper you and not to harm you, plans to give you hope and a future. Then you will call upon me and come and pray to me, and I will listen to you. You will seek me and find me when you seek me with all your heart." (*Jeremiah 29:11-13 NIV)

There is no doubt that the amount of prayer increases during an awakening. The intimacy that people have with God increases, and they respond to Him through prayer.

Prayer being a characteristic of a revival is fairly obvious, but what is more interesting is to look at what happens leading up to revival. There are generally two types of prayer - organised and travailing.

Organised prayer for revival occurs in churches all over the country from time to time. There are even calls for such prayer in stadiums; the belief being that the more we ask or beg the Lord for revival, the quicker revival will come. As already mentioned, it has not worked and I do not believe it is meant to work like that.

> *"I am going to send you what my Father has promised; but stay in the city until you have been clothed with power from on high."* (Luke 24:49 NIV)

Jesus does not tell the disciples to go to Jerusalem to pray, He just tells them to wait. I do not think that prayer is very effective if it is done out of duty or out of obedience to a leader. I can almost hear the cries of outrage from people disagreeing with this statement! We are called to pray, and we pray about many things, but I believe that the most effective prayers are those that the Lord puts on our hearts.

Effective prayer comes from the presence of God. I believe that Travailing Prayer has a big influence on revival, being the intercessor's response to God's decision and message that it is time for revival.

The following are examples of the impact of Travailing Prayer on revivals of the past, that I believe highlight the power and necessity for it.

Great Awakening (1738-?)

The further one goes back in history, the more difficult it is to understand the Church language of that time and equate it to our terminology today. Looking for clear examples of Travailing Prayer in the eighteenth century is not easy as they do not often use this term. In my opinion, when they wrote about 'wrestling' or other such words. they were describing travail.

Although I have read a great deal about the Great Awakening I have, as yet, found no record of prayer meetings calling for revival in the late 1730's. However, Count Zinzendorf began a 24/7 prayer meeting in 1727, in Hernhut, Germany that went on for a hundred years. I suspect that they were travailing and I think it credible that their prayers helped start the Great Awakening.

The huge Awakening that hit our nation occurred three or four years later than the one that began through Jonathan Edwards in the United States. I found this quote by Charles Finney, that shows they were travailing at that time.

> "I have never known a person sweat blood; but I have known a person pray till the blood started from his nose. And I have known persons pray till they were all wet with perspiration, in the coldest weather in winter. I have known persons pray for hours, till their strength was all exhausted with the agony of their minds. Such prayers prevailed with God. This agony in prayer was prevalent in Jonathan Edwards' day, in the revivals which then took place."[3]

This, together with the few accounts below convince me that Travailing Prayer was at the heart of the Methodist revivals of that century.

The following is a very interesting account written in 1767. John Valton was one of John Wesley's early itinerant preachers.

> "On examining my heart, I have found in myself three kinds of prayer: first, an impetuous, earnest, and violent desire that others might be blessed ; that is chiefly man's prayer: secondly, an humble, earnest,

pleading prayer, proceeding from a broken heart, bleeding with compassion; there is much of the Spirit of God in this, it is generally much blessed to others: thirdly, the prayer of God, or praying in the Holy Ghost. This consists in short phrases and sentences, chiefly in Scripture language; the soul feasts on the answer while one petition slowly succeeds another. This is the prayer which God emphatically inspires. It is often not relished by lukewarm professors; but on the purified it leaves behind the mantle of Elijah. Lord, evermore teach me thus to pray!"[4]

Valton was only twenty-seven years old at the time and it is reasonable to assume that people around him were praying in the same way. I believe his first type of prayer is 'petition' prayer, the second 'travailing' and the third something else. A dear friend of mine who is an intercessor, told me that she has prayed like this in the past; waiting on the Lord until a Bible verse or something else came to mind, then praying it briefly before waiting on the Lord again, and so on.

John Wesley organised his followers, first into Circuits that could include three or four counties, then into Societies (like churches), then into Classes and Bands. The Class and Band would equate with our home groups today. You had to be invited to join a Class and prove that you were someone who was passionate and chasing after God. There was a lot of prayer going on in these Classes, the aim of which was to go from glory to glory and I believe that most of this prayer was travail. The Classes were the engine rooms of the Societies.

In 1781 John Valton wrote:

> "I was at Dawgreen, the southern part of the town of Dewsbury. Being alone in my chamber, I prostrated myself before the Lord, to ask the outpouring of His Spirit on so populous a neighbourhood, while my eyes were suffused with tears. I then came

down to engage in family prayer; and the power of God fell upon me, enabling me to pray with much enlargement, as the Spirit gave me utterance. I had a blessed revival before my eyes, and we praised God by way of anticipation; for I was fully assured the Lord was about to work. My petitions were uttered in the assurance of faith; for I knew that God would make bare His holy arm. The family felt the Divine unction; and I continued till I could scarcely rise from my knees. I went upstairs; but could engage in no work, except prayer and praise."[5]

This is an excellent example of Travailing Prayer birthing revival as a significant revival began shortly afterwards.

This account of Travailing Prayer from 1757 resulted in a violent man coming to know Jesus. Alexander Mather was another of Wesley's preachers.

"At Matthew Bagshaw's I found John Johnson, of York, who said, 'I am glad you are come; for here is a poor man, who is to die to-morrow, whose behaviour is terrifying: he curses, swears, and threatens death to all that have given evidence against him; the jailer in particular. He will see no clergyman, but says he resolves to be a devil, that he may revenge himself. The minister has given me free leave to visit him. I went this morning; but he said, 'Give yourself no trouble about me. By this time tomorrow I shall be a devil, and then I will come and tear that villain in pieces.' We immediately went to prayer, and vehemently wrestled with God on his behalf. After prayer, we went to him, and at first sight observed an entire change in his behaviour. We inquired when this sudden change began, and found it was just while we were at prayer."[6]

In 1758 a national revival began in Otley, Yorkshire. The

following testimony is how it began. This meeting was a typical Methodist Class meeting and it clearly shows people travailing and that the result was revival.

> "On Friday, February 13th, about thirty persons were met together at Otley, about eight o'clock in the evening, in order (as usual) to pray, and sing hymns, and provoke one another to love and good works. After prayer was ended, when they proceeded to speak of the several states of their souls, some, with deep sighs and groans, complained of the burden they felt for the remains of in-dwelling sin; seeing in a clearer light than ever before, the necessity of a deliverance from it.
>
> When they had spent the usual time together, a few went to their own houses; but the rest remained upon their knees, groaning for the fulfilment of the great and precious promises of God. One being desired to pray, he no sooner began to lift up his voice to God, then the Holy Ghost made intercession in all that were present, with groanings that could not be uttered. At length the travail of their souls burst out into loud and ardent cries. They had no doubt of the favour of God, but they could not rest, while there was anything in them contrary to His nature. One cried out, in an exceeding great agony, 'Lord deliver me from my sinful nature!' Then a second, a third, and fourth. And while the person who prayed first, was calling upon God in these words, 'Thou God of Abraham, Isaac, and Jacob, hear us for the sake of thy Son Jesus!' one was heard to say, 'Blessed be the Lord God for ever, for He hath cleansed my heart.' Another and another spoke the like experience, and the writer thus concludes: Thus they continued for the space of two hours; some praising and magnifying God, some crying to Him for pardon or purity of heart, with the greatest agony of spirit."[7]

During this revival Wesley began to recognise the importance of prayer meetings as a means for bringing about revival. In a letter to John Wesley from Alexander Mather, who was pastoring a revival of his own in 1760, he writes:

> "As I wrote to you the most minute circumstances of the work, and you were there in the very height of it, you judged it best to place me in the Circuit another year. But I made a false step in the beginning of it. Longing for peace and preferring the judgment of other men to my own, I agreed that my wife should not hold any more prayer-meetings. Immediately the work began to decay, both as to its swiftness and extensiveness. And though I continued to insist as strongly as ever upon the same points, yet there was not the same effect, for want of seconding by prayer-meetings the blow which was given in preaching."[8]

Around 1770 there is this account by James Rogers, another of Wesley's itinerant preachers, who had been seeking Sanctification for a considerable time and then someone travailed for him.

> "That pious family no sooner learned my errand than they encouraged me to expect the blessing that hour and exhorted me to believe on the Lord Jesus for full salvation. We then fell on our knees and a good woman full of faith and love wrestled and pleaded with the Lord for me. In less than fifteen minutes my burden was removed and I felt an entire change."[9]

Robert Lomas, yet another of Wesley's preachers, wrote in 1793 from Greetland, Halifax. He was conducting a love-feast where he gave testimony to receiving Sanctification. Travailing Prayer then began and revival came.

> "In the love-feast I bore my feeble testimony to the truth, and spoke explicitly of my own experience;

saying, for some time I have found nothing contrary to the love of God and man, and as far as I know, the Lord has cleansed me from all sin; but of this I want a clearer witness. What was said seemed to have a good effect upon the people in general, they were evidently stirred up to lay hold upon the Lord. I was desirous to spend a little time in prayer and requested several of the brethren to use their liberty. They did so, pleading with God for themselves and others. I found myself uncommonly affected while one of them was praying for me. With my whole heart, with all the powers of my soul and body, I then cried to the Lord for a general blessing. As I prayed and pleaded, my faith was strengthened, and I said, 'Oh Lord, if it will not displease thee, we would wrestle with thee, as Jacob did; and with Jacob thou wast not displeased'. Immediately my whole frame felt the power of God, and the whole house seemed filled with his glory. I continued praying, or rather praising God. My soul was lost and swallowed up in him. I had before been blessed in a similar way; but never in that degree." The people were amazed, some glorified God; meanwhile the gracious influences waxed stronger and stronger, each individual felt to forget everything, save their eternal interests. The world receded from their view, Satan lost his hold, evil agencies found nowhere whereon to fasten; faith being strongly exercised, a wrestling spirit filled every heart, while every power both of body and mind seemed to be engaged. Then the gates of heaven were opened, the glory of the Holy One of Israel filling the very place, and by some now living and by hundreds transplanted to paradise, Greetland Lovefeast will never be forgotten."[10]

Great Yorkshire Revival (1794)

William Bramwell was also a Methodist itinerant preacher,

who was well known for his powerful praying.

> "But it was in the exercise of prayer that he (Bramwell) was deemed most remarkable. This, his peculiar gift, was developed at that early period of his ministry with extraordinary power; and from the results which accrued, many persons were disposed to impute even a kind of supernatural efficacy to his petitions. On one occasion, whilst employed in supplication at a meeting, it appeared to the assembly as if the Spirit had descended upon them like a flash of lightning streaming into the apartment: all present were strangely moved, and to one penitent heart the visitation was said to have carried the evidences of Divine forgiveness. At other times they would fancy that the glory of God filled the room during his addresses to heaven, and that 'the boards even trembled beneath them!'"[11]

It is not a coincidence that revival began in most of the churches where Bramwell was posted – Travailing Prayer ignited the revivals. He is known as the leader of the 'Great Yorkshire Revival', but the first revival he was involved in was in Dewsbury two years earlier in 1792.

> "Prayer meetings were established in the morning, and at the early hour of five o'clock, many met to aid him in petitioning for the desired Pentecost. An able assistant was found in a pious woman then visiting the neighbourhood, Ann Cutler. Well did she vindicate her title to the appellation of "Praying Nanny." By four o'clock in the morning this enthusiastic creature would rise, and plead with all her energy on behalf of the parched and desolate Church. In another apartment not far distant, the deep earnest tones of the young preacher's voice might at the same moment be heard in an 'agony' of intercession for the same blessing."[12]

Ann Cutler was a truly remarkable person, a most anointed travailer whom William Bramwell believed was responsible for the Great Yorkshire revival. She came to the Lord in 1785, dedicating her life to a relationship with God. She had an overwhelming burden for the lost. She would frequently say, "I think I must pray. I cannot be happy unless I cry for sinners. I do not want any praise; I want nothing but souls to be brought to God. I am reproached by most. I cannot do it to be seen or heard of men. I see the world going to destruction, and I am burdened till I pour out my soul to God for them."[13]

She prayed without ceasing; her life was a life of prayer. She wrote.

> "I spoke to a large company in the open air in Ricks' garden. The word given was Genesis 46:1. The Lord came down in the power of His spirit; many old grey-headed sinners were brought upon their knees and cried aloud for mercy. Oh, it was a most blessed sight! God knows that I 'did travail in birth' for souls here. I had the 'desire of my heart' given - seeking, inquiring souls stopped me in the streets as I passed. Holy God! Let thy kingdom come and bind the whole earth to thy sway. Amen."[14]

She began to go from church to church. In 1792 she joined Bramwell in Dewsbury. William Bramwell gives a detailed account of the revival.

> "Our first year was a year of hard labour and much grief. Nanny Cutler joined us in continual prayer to God for a revival of His work. As I was praying in my room I received an answer from God in a particular way, and had the revival discovered to me in its manner and effects. I had no more doubt. I could say, 'The Lord will come; I know He will come, and that suddenly.'

Nothing appeared very particular, till under Nanny Cutler's prayer one soul received a clean heart. We were confident that the Lord would do the same for others. At a prayer meeting two found peace with God; and the same week two more received the same blessing. On the Monday evening the Bands met. A remarkable spirit of prayer was given to the people. several, who were the most prejudiced, were suddenly struck, and in agonies groaned for deliverance.

The work continued almost in every meeting; and sixty persons in and about Dewsbury received sanctification and walked in that liberty. Our love feasts began to be crowded and people from every neighbouring circuit visited us. Great numbers found pardon, and some perfect love. They went home and declared what God had done for them.

…Ann Cutler went to Leeds circuit, and though vital religion had been very low, the Lord made use of her at the beginning of a revival, and the work spread nearly through the circuit. Very often ten or twenty, or more, were saved in a meeting.

Wherever she went there was an amazing power of God attending her prayers."[15]

Sadly, Ann Cutler died in 1796, after only eleven years of serving the Lord.

Primitive Methodists Revivals

The Primitive Methodists began their existence holding camp meetings in 1810 where many were saved. These would take place in a field, where they would place around three preaching platforms and where members would gather together in groups to pray that the visitors would receive salvation. One of the founders relates what their Travailing Prayer was like.

"The Micheldever Society constituted one of the praying companies; and they prayed until it seemed as if heaven and earth were brought together. At first, I trembled lest their fervency should enrage the persecutors; but there was no remedy; it was impossible to restrain them. I then joined with them, and felt perfectly free to live or die; and, contrary to our expectation, when we returned to the preaching stand for the second course of sermons, the vast concourse of people stood as if they were entranced; the preachers had extraordinary liberty, and the word was indeed with power; the people in prayer, wrestled with God and prevailed, and the song of praise seemed to make the place a paradise. The entire day's services were brought to a close in peace; and the impressions made were unquestionably such as never will be forgotten by the multitudes who were present on that memorable day.

This powerful meeting gave a mighty impetus to 'the kingdom of heaven,' in the county of Hampshire. The infant churches, which had been recently planted in the various surrounding villages, were greatly invigorated; while the hard moral soil of those neighbourhoods, which had hitherto violently resisted our entrance into them, and which was so much in harmony with the flinty character of the material soil of the same localities, was, in several instances, softened into 'good ground,' to receive the 'good seed' of the 'glorious Gospel of the blessed God.'"[16]

At some point it was noticed that the power of the camp-meetings was declining. It was also noticed that the composition of those meetings had changed. To begin with, they were made up of numerous, powerful prayer meetings and short talks, but the talks became longer and longer; sometimes two hours, so there was less time for praying. Once the balance was corrected, the power returned. We can certainly learn a lesson from this.

Charles Finney and Daniel Nash

I usually only like to give examples from the United Kingdom, but Finney and Nash are exceptional. My only excuse is that Finney did come over to minister here. They ministered together mainly in New York state in the late 1820's. Nash would always go to the town a couple of weeks before the meetings to travail and then Finney would hold the meetings and revivals would begin.

> "During the Rochester (New York) meetings there are several accounts of two men in deep agony of soul while praying day and night. Some accounts name Nash, some Clary, others both. It seems they were together in fasting and prayer much of the time, weeping and crying out to God. Sometimes they lay prostrate without strength to stand up. Their concern over sinners being lost brought great stress to their minds and souls. They groaned under the load, they risked health and gave up comforts that the battle of the heavenlies might be won. Sometimes they "would writhe and groan in agony" over souls. God honoured their burden-bearing and sent revival. Privately they prayed and publicly God answered. "Practically everyone in the city was converted. The only theatre in the city was converted into a livery stable, the only circus into a soap and candle factory, and the grog shops (bars and taverns) were closed."[17]

> "Finney always preached with the expectation of seeing the Holy Spirit suddenly outpoured. Until this happened little or nothing was accomplished. But the moment the Spirit fell upon the people, He had nothing else to do but point them to the Lamb of God.

Thus he lived and wrought for years in an atmosphere of revival."[18]

Finney describing what Nash did:

"The plain truth of the matter is that the Spirit leads a man to pray; and if God leads a man to pray for an individual, the inference from the Bible is, that God designs to save that individual. If we find, by comparing our state of mind with the Bible, that we are led by the Spirit to pray for an individual, we have good evidence to believe that God is prepared to bless him.

Such praying required mental effort to aim at the proper effect with true soul struggle. To move from real burden to solid faith often requires the path of soul agony. We are too committed to cop out with fatalism, unconcern, or shifting the responsibility to the lost. It may require a wrestling in prayer until we obtain the desired blessing. This is on a far higher plane than the physical. These struggles of soul and spirit may produce more than weariness in the physical realm."[19]

Kilsyth Revival (1839)

William Burns was the minister in Kilsyth in 1839 when there was a large revival. He wrote about the beginning of the revival:

"Some of the people of God who had been longing and wrestling for a time of refreshing from the Lord's presence, and who had during much the previous night, been travailing in birth for souls, came to the meeting, not only with the hope, but with well-nigh anticipation of God's glorious appearing from the impressions they had upon their own souls of

Jehovah's approaching glory and majesty."

1859-62 Revival

This was the biggest revival the United Kingdom has experienced with an estimated 1.1 million salvations. I believe this revival was also birthed through Travailing Prayer.

In November 1856, a young man called James McQuilikin gave his life to Jesus. In September 1857 McQulikin and three young friends who had also recently come to the Lord (two through James), decided to meet together once a week at the old school room at Kells in Northern Ireland for prayer and Bible study.

Interestingly, Jeremiah Lamphier, began to pray for revival in New York City during the same month the four young men started praying in Ulster. The Lord had told Lamphier to pray for an hour each day at lunchtime for revival; these meetings grew exponentially until a million were saved in America during 1857-58. The revival did not start in the United Kingdom until 1859.

In his book on the revival, Ian Paisley wrote:

> "These young converts were convinced of three great fundamentals and upon these their prayer and fellowship meeting was based. They believed in the Sovereignty of the Holy Spirit, the Sufficiency of the Holy Scripture, and the Secret of Holy Supplication."[20]

One of the four young men described the prayer meetings:

> "We did not allow the unsaved in the prayer meeting. It was a fellowship meeting of Christians met for the one great object of praying for an outpouring of the Holy Spirit upon ourselves and upon the surrounding

country. This was the one great object and burden of our prayers. We held right to the one thing and did not run off to anything else… the Lord knew what we wanted and we kept right on praying until the power came."[21]

As new converts they were passionate young men hoping to pray in a revival. Add to that the term 'Holy Supplication' and the words from the testimony above; I have little doubt that they practiced Travailing Prayer in their efforts to pull heaven down to earth.

In fact prayer brought about revival in hundreds of towns around the United Kingdom. I have discovered through reports I have read something I have not come across before, the 'Spirit of Prayer' prevailed across the UK. There were several reports of people, including children feeling 'compelled' by Holy Spirit to pray and reports of amazed pastors who heard new believers pray with extraordinary eloquence and passion and with a real belief that their prayers would be answered.

A Spirit of Prayer is when Holy Spirit gives you a particular unction to pray. It may be on an individual or a corporate body.

"In the present movement we have been greatly struck by the fact that so much of the spirit of prayer has possessed the Lord's people. They draw the heaven of heavens, as it were, into every prayer-meeting; hence such congregations as were never before seen are brought to¬gether on these occasions. But, in every one of them, there is something more than a large congregation—the prayers penetrate the hearts of those who attend, whether they be male or female, even persons who never scarcely attended a place of worship are impressed."

Welsh Revival (1904-5)

The Welsh Revival was full of Travailing Prayer before and during the meetings.

Although Evan Roberts was not 'The' leader of the 1904 Welsh Revival, as newspapers would have you believe, he was an important part of it and he was an intercessor.

In the weeks that preceded the beginning of the revival in Loughor, Swansea, Roberts spent hours every day before the Lord. Sometimes he just could not explain where the time had gone, it was as if at one moment it was 10.00pm and the next, 11.00pm. He was experiencing 'the purest joy on earth'. He 'prayed, wept and sighed for a great spiritual awakening' always asking heaven for salvations.

During the services at Loughor he travailed with extraordinary intensity, which in quite a short time wore him out. The meetings had very little of the 'word' in them; they were mainly occupied with prayer.

> "Some people cannot understand why he does not pray in the meetings, and criticise him accordingly. It would be well for such to bear in mind that no one supplicates more than he does, although he does not do so audibly. I have seen him engaged in silent prayer in the pulpit for an hour and a half. When quiet and his face buried in his hands, as a rule, he is then praying, and praying so fervently, and with such earnestness, that it tells on his whole constitution. Because of this, the meetings in which he speaks but little, cost him very dearly. They often leave him in a weakened state. Yes, he prays a great deal in the meetings, and I have often been awe-struck with his strange intensity, as I stood near him. At times he stands in the pulpit, leaning on the Bible; but the only

intimation we get that he is praying is to see his lips moving."[22]

Also during meetings in this revival, often intercessors would stand up in the middle of the meeting and implore the heavens; endeavouring to pull heaven down to earth. These people were much valued by their churches as their effectiveness was recognised.

Here is an example of Travailing Prayer during the revival.

> "There were more people coming to the weekly meetings, and a greater willingness to take part in them. Young people showed more of a desire than previously for the work of religion, and it was easier to get hold of them. Soon the spirit of prayer began to fall on us, and all the ordinary week-day meetings had to give place to the prayer meeting. Our hearts burned within us as we heard the young people communing with God, begging him to strengthen some relative or friend or neighbour so they might come to religion."[23]

Hebrides Revival 1949-52

The Hebrides Revival is another revival that was birthed in prayer.

Both the Church of Scotland and the Free Church in Lewis put out a call to their people to pray for revival. The island had a culture of prayer and there had been several revivals there in the past, particularly in 1939. So, the island went to prayer and amongst them were two sisters, both in their eighties and one blind.

> "These women prayed for revival twice a week - on Tuesdays from 10.00pm to approx. 3.00am - and one of them had a vision of the church full of young

people. They called for their minister and told him he needed to organise prayer in a barn twice a week while they prayed at home. Recognising that these women walked close to God, he did as they said. For six weeks they prayed until a young man declared that the prayers were wasted unless they were right with God. "Then he lifted his two hands and prayed, 'God, are my hands clean? Is my heart pure?' But he got no further. That young man fell to his knees and then fell in a trance and lay on the floor of the barn. And in the words of the minister, at that moment, he and his other office bearers were gripped by the conviction that a God-sent revival must always be related to Holiness, must ever be related to Godliness. Are my hands clean? Is my heart pure?

When that happened in the barn, the power of God swept into the parish and an awareness of God gripped the community. On the following day the looms were silent, little work was done on the farms as men and women gave themselves to thinking on eternal things, gripped by eternal realities."[24]

The sisters knew that Duncan Campbell was the man to lead the revival, but when invited to come he refused. Undeterred the women continued to pray as they knew he was meant to come and indeed he did.

One town in Lewis was not responding to prayer for revival. Arnol is two miles from Barvas and extra prayer was called for, so Duncan Campbell and others went to have an extended prayer meeting in someone's house.

"It was a hard battle as one after another attempted to break through in prayer. Sometime after midnight Duncan Campbell called upon John Smith (a leading intercessor on the island) to pray. He had not prayed all night. He rose and prayed for some time and then he said, 'Lord, I do not know how Mr. Campbell or any of these other men stand with you, but if I know my own heart, I know that I am thirsty. You have promised to pour water on him that is thirsty. If You don't do it, how can I ever believe You again. Your honour is at stake. You are a covenant-keeping God. Fulfil Your covenant engagement.' It was a prayer of a man who was walking with God. At that moment the house shook."[25]

Two unsaved neighbours who were listening were saved that night. The meeting had ended and on leaving the house they saw people carrying chairs to the meeting hall, expectant of a revival meeting. The revival in Arnol had begun.

Duncan Campbell once said:

"I could take you to a little cottage in the Hebrides and introduce you to a young woman. She is not educated; but I have known that young woman to pray heaven into a community, to pray power into a meeting. I have known that young woman to be so caught in the power of the Holy Ghost that men and women around her were made to tremble."[26]

There are many examples above of Travailing Prayer bringing about revival and individual salvation. I am now going to cover the subject of Travailing Prayer being used by individuals to break through for personal revival.

Chapter Three

Travail for Personal Revival

From my research I have noticed that from 1738-1952 every one of the hundreds of accounts of salvation I have read occurred in roughly the same way. To begin with they were convicted by Holy Spirit of how sinful they were; their sins became so real to them and they would normally cry out for mercy. Many would weep during this process. If in church, there would normally be somebody who would pray with the person, praying that they saw Jesus as the answer. They would also explain to the person what they were experiencing. There would then be an interval of maybe a few minutes or some years before they realised that Jesus was the answer and He could forgive their sins. Most of them then had an encounter with God and would feel Holy Spirit flood their souls.

Before including some testimonies showing this experience I would like to point out that a reason for including this section is that I am puzzled that this scenario rarely happens these days. Most often during the last few decades people have given their lives to Jesus by coming to the front of church and repeating a ninety second prayer spoken by the minister. Most have not had any conviction of sin and no encounter with God. Why did the conversion experience change? I do not know and I shall probably have to do a reprint of this booklet when I find out. All I know is that I never had an encounter when I came to the Lord, but I wish I had.

Here are some testimonies.

The first took place in a school in Coleraine during the 1859 revival.

> A boy had just testified to his salvation, then, "the attention of the whole school was attracted. Boy after boy silently slipped out of the room. After a while, the master stood on something that enabled him to look over the wall of the playground. There he saw a number of boys ranged round the wall on their knees in earnest prayer, every one separate. The scene overcame him. Presently he turned to the pupil who had already been a comforter to Sean, and said, 'Do you think you can go and pray with these boys?' He went out, and kneeling down among them, began to implore the Lord to forgive their sins, for the sake of Him who had borne all upon the cross. Their silent grief soon broke into a bitter cry. As this reached the ears of the boys in the room, it seemed to pierce their hearts, as by one consent they cast themselves upon their knees and began to cry for mercy. The girls' school was above, and the cry no sooner penetrated to their room than, hearing in it a call to themselves, they too, fell upon their knees and wept. Strange disorder for schoolmaster and mistress to have to control!

> The united cry reached the adjoining streets. Every ear, prepared by the Spirit, at once interpreted it as the voice of those seeking Jesus. One after another the neighbours came in, and at once cast themselves upon their knees and joined in the cry for mercy."

This cry for mercy was the boys travailing in prayer, as was the praying of the boy for his friends. How many of them found Jesus is unknown.

This is an account of a revival in Shepton Mallet in 1767 written by John Valton. It is a good example of the stages people went through. The term 'awakened' means that they were awakened to their sin (convicted by Holy Spirit) which is why revival is often and more accurately called an awakening. Finding peace with God means they received Christ into their lives.

"Many, I perceived, were affected and wept bitterly under the word. I met the Society, but the crowd stayed behind and I thought more than once that we should have had a general cry. When I came down from the pulpit I found many in great distress and could not leave them without prayer. Mr Coulson told me afterwards that he believed about one hundred persons, were more or less, awakened under that discourse.

In the beginning of November, I spent two or three nights with that people and many seemed truly convinced and earnest for salvation. The mornings I spent in my lodgings to receive and advise those who came in distress, enquiring what must they do to be saved. The congregations increased every night and a general spirit of alarm and enquiry was spread through the town and neighbourhood. That week many found peace and forty-four were admitted on trial into the society.

In my next visit, I had another wonderful night and returned thanks for about twenty-two that had lately found peace with God. The preachers in the Circuit had fostered and encouraged the work. I may truly say, I never saw such a general awakening and without the least appearance of wildfire. One morning I think not less than twenty came to my chamber in distress and two of them found peace with God.'"[27]

Here is another account from the 1859 revival, this time from Bovevagh, Northern Ireland.

"When the usual time for public worship came, the church was so crowded that we were obliged to retire to the churchyard and conduct the services in the open air. The crowd became immense, the minister and congregation of Scriggan having joined us, and a more solemn assembly never met on earth.

During the services, the tears and suppressed sobs of many showed that it was no ordinary occasion - that it was the day of God's power - that the Spirit of power was dealing personally with men's souls. When the benediction was pronounced, a few retired, but the great majority lingered - stood, in fact, as if held in a vice, or bound with a chain - and in a moment, as if struck with a thunderbolt, about a hundred persons were prostrated on their knees, sending forth a wail from hearts bruised, broken, and overwhelmed with horror, such as will never be forgotten, and which, perhaps, for solemnity and awe, will never be surpassed until the judgment-day. Oh, what must the wailings of the lost in hell be, when the discovery is made that their lamps are gone out, that the day of mercy is past, and the door of hope shut forever! For hours these stricken, smitten, bleeding souls remained on their bended knees, unconscious of everything but their own guilt and danger, and need of a Saviour, pleading and praying with an intensity and fervour which surpasses all description...

...Numbers of cases of conviction of a very interesting nature took place in private, in the family, or elsewhere. Some were struck with a sense of sin in the field, when working - some on the highway - some when conducting family worship, and others in their beds. One person told me, when he awoke in the morning he found his pillow wet with tears, and his whole frame feeble and exhausted. One strong young man, when working alone in a turf bog, was prostrated with a spade in his hand, and for hours he there wrestled in prayer to God, and all the succeeding night, in his house, the cry for mercy went up from a broken heart. It was not till the morning he found peace, when his powerful muscular frame was shaken and exhausted, as if he had been rising out of a protracted and severe fever."[28]

Finally, a report from the 1921 Fisherman's Revival, the last revival we have had in England. This revival came about, indirectly, from Travailing Prayer. Douglas Brown was a popular minister in Balham and after being asked to hold revival meetings in Lowestoft early in March, he spent four months wrestling with God. He came to a point where he was prepared to give up his church when the Glory of God broke through and he received the Baptism of Fire. This transformed him and it was the power and authority that he received in that Baptism that brought about the revival just four days later.

Hugh Ferguson, who invited Brown, reported on a meeting that took place on the first Thursday of the revival.

"The inquiry room was packed a few minutes after the sermon, with men and women crying out to God, 'What must I do to be saved?' It was like an auction room. There was my brother the Rev John Hayes, Vicar of Christ Church, dealing with anxious souls, and the Rev John Edwards of Brixton standing on another form and I was standing with some others, and we were all engaged in the glorious work of pointing men and women to Christ. The place was so packed that when you got in you could not alter your position. 'You will have to come to Christ where you are.' That night they were coming to Jesus all over the building."[29]

The inquiry room mentioned here was where people convicted of their sin in the meeting were sent to seek Jesus.

Chapter Four

Contemporary Testimonies

The following testimony took place at the end of 2018 amongst a native people group who were very poor and who had experienced much hardship. My friend recounted what happened:

"It was one of the most holy things I have ever experienced in my life. When I first arrived there I felt the fear of the Lord restraining me to be very very careful with the people. I was not allowed to do anything but wait on the Lord because it was a Sovereign restraint. The first night the Lord had me speak to them on Regal identity in Christ. It was a beautiful evening, Holy Spirit began to move, real affirmation and healing were flowing.

The next night it was packed and the fear of the Lord was on me again. As the worship started I went down on the floor and went under a spirit of holiness. I began to repent; some of it was identificational for the people, and it was also very personal, over any level of self-striving (where it was me who was ministering and not Holy Spirit) and where I hadn't got out of the way. I was repenting and repenting and repenting for any attitudes that were contrary to the nature of God. I was in this place of deep groaning and repentance when I had an amazing encounter with the Lord.

To the right of me I saw Holy Spirit as a person dressed in a long brown garment representing humility. I was completely undone. I was crying and I was a mess. I then felt a release to start speaking about the vision I was experiencing and invited people to come to kneel in the River. People came to the front, and kneeling down they began wailing, crying and repenting; getting their lives right with the Lord. Grown men were coming down crying and screaming, coming under conviction of sin. It was a Holy mess. I took my hands off the meeting and let God be God.

I spoke a bit more of my message and then I began ministering to people, touching them really, really gently and each one would fly out onto the floor under the power of God. Then all the children started to come and started repenting from sin. It went on for hours. I ended up sitting on the stage, watching Holy Spirit at work. This outpouring literally burst out of travail and repentance."

The revival carried on after my friend left.

The following is a testimony from a substitute teacher of six to seven-year olds.

"As a substitute teacher I found that engaging the children became not only a job but an intercessory assignment from the Lord. The first two years in the class room I made a point to pray during each recess and lunch break. A growing burden for the children weighed on me as I observed and learned of the challenges they faced and the obvious battle with darkness that pursued them. An increasing sense of love and desperation for these children began to burn in me.

An opportunity for me to live alone presented itself, which then gave me the opportunity to avail myself to hours of daily uninterrupted prayer. My mornings before school began with 1-2 hours of praying in tongues which usually lead me into a deep groaning, often overcome with travail. I could feel The Father's yearning for these young ones, and also His fierce roar. There was deep weeping (sometimes wailing) followed by what felt to be the zeal of holy vengeance against the demonic realm. This mode of intercession would leave me drenched with sweat, but fully charged with the Holy Spirit. I hungered deeply to see true salvation and deliverance come to these children.

Then one day it happened. I stepped into a class room and was calling role. I addressed a little boy with the name Gabrielle. I felt the hovering presence of the Holy Spirit and asked if anyone happened to know who Gabrielle in the Bible was. This launched me into twenty minutes of a preaching anointing that gripped me unlike any public manifestation I had ever known before. At the end of this time, I explained that Jesus' greatest desire is to live in our hearts and that He enters in when we invite Him. A young boy asked if we could do that now! I closed my eyes and opened my hands to the Lord, and without telling them to repeat after me, they instinctively followed my words. A heavenly being was to my left, I could feel it's strong presence. Later I would learn that this was a salvation angel. I lead them through a prayer for salvation, deliverance and to receive the baptism of the Holy Spirit. I wanted to take them as far as possible in the little time I had available. The children began to chatter and tell each other that they were feeling heat in their bellies. There was such joy in the room!

Since I was substitute teaching, I never had a chance to revisit this particular class room. However, the Lord assured me that He had marked these children and they are His. This day was the first day of many, many that would have a similar theme over the next seven years. As the travail continued, and as I availed myself to the labour of birthing souls, there seemed to be a momentum of fruitfulness that continued until my time as a teacher was completed. I have found that there is nothing quite like the pain and the joy of intercession...and the glory of satisfying the longing heart of the King"

What wonderful examples of the power and blessing of Travailing Prayer.

The same intercessor who gave this testimony also told me how she is part of a group of invited people who gather together to pray for their nation or for situations to shift. This is not a small group, sometimes two hundred attend and she has experienced times of group travailing. The Spirit of God comes over the whole group and together they travail in prayer, groaning and weeping for a situation. She will sometimes see in the paper the next day or next week a change in the situation they had been travailing over

Chapter Five

Conclusion

Here are three quotes on Travailing Prayer.

"At God's counter there are no 'SALE DAYS,' for the price of revival is ever the same - TRAVAIL." Leonard Ravenhill

"Storm the throne of grace and persevere therein, and mercy will come down." John Wesley

"The prayer that prevails is not the work of lips and fingertips. It is the cry of a broken heart and the travail of a stricken soul." Samuel Chadwick (Wesleyan minister)

Having read all these reports and testimonies on Travailing Prayer, I hope you can see the importance of it and its connection with revival. Story after story, testimony after testimony has shown that revivals are birthed in travail.

Someone said to me that she thought that compassion was linked to the womb of God, that brings about a birth. This makes sense to me; perhaps seeing compassion in us God burdens our hearts and then we birth His plan through travail.

As mentioned though there can be a cost; travailing can be painful, exhausting etc, so we need to be wise and we need to do it only when the Lord leads us. We must also be careful not to remain in travail for longer than the Lord wants as one might take the feelings into our soul rather than releasing them back to the Lord.

God never promised us a trouble-free existence; in fact, we are told to take up our cross daily. How amazing it is to think that our travail can bring about amazing breakthroughs and even revival!

The United Kingdom needs people to rise up and open their hearts to being used by the Lord to help Him bring His plans and purposes to this nation. We have not had revival in England for nearly a hundred years, please let it not be another hundred before we see the United Kingdom transformed.

End Notes

1. The Elijah List 21, January 2005.
2. Intercessory Prayer, by Dutch Sheets, page 111.
3. Lectures on Revival in Religion, by Charles Finney, page 52.
4. Lives of Early Methodist Preachers, by Thomas Jackson, Volume 6, page 65.
5. Lives of Early Methodist Preachers, by Thomas Jackson, Volume 6, page 101.
6. Lives of Early Methodist Preachers, by Thomas Jackson, Volume 2, page 156-7.
7. Wesley's Journal, 16th February, 1760.
8. Lives of Early Methodist Preachers, by Thomas Jackson, Volume 2, page 180-81.
9. Lives of Early Methodist Preachers, by Thomas Jackson, Volume 4, page 290.
10. History of Wesleyan Methodism in Halifax and its vicinity, by J U Walker, page 190.
11. Memoir of the life and ministry of William Bramwell, by William Bramwell and his family, published in 1848, page 39-40.
12. Memoir of the life and ministry of William Bramwell', by William Bramwell and his family, published in 1848, page 39-40.
13. A short account of the Life and Death of Ann Cutler, by William Bramwell, 1796.
14. A short account of the Life and Death of Ann Cutler, by William Bramwell, 1796.
15. A short account of the Life and Death of Ann Cutler, by William Bramwell, 1796.
16. The History of the Primitive Methodist Connexion from its Origin, by John Petty, 1860, page 274-5.
17. http://sentinellenehemie.free.fr/jpreno1_gb.html
18. http://sentinellenehemie.free.fr/jpreno1_gb.html
19. http://sentinellenehemie.free.fr/jpreno1_gb.html
20. The '59 Revival, by Ian R K Paisley, Chapter 2.
21. The '59 Revival, by Ian R K Paisley, Chapter 2.

22.   Evan Roberts, by D M Phillips, Chapter 13.
23.   Goleuad Newspaper, 7th April 1905 – Llanbedr
24.   Duncan Campbell, taped sermon 1968.
25.   Sounds from Heaven, by Colin and Mary Peckham, page 113.
26.   The Price and Power of Revival, sermon by Duncan Campbell.
27.   Lives of Early Methodist Preachers, by Thomas Jackson, Volume 6, page 125-6.
28.   The Banner of Ulster, 21st June 1859.
29.   A Forgotten Revival, by Stanley C Griffin, pages 23-4

MICHAEL MARCEL'S OTHER BOOKS

This book records the nine most significant revivals/awakenings that took place in the United Kingdom over the last 400 years. It is very important to know the exciting stories of the amazing things God has done in the UK that is part of our spiritual heritage.

We can be set on fire by reading the stories and wonderful testimonies of people who experienced the power of God. They will excite you and give you a vision of how to light fires of revival in your area!

This book is available through www.ukwells.org

MICHAEL MARCEL'S OTHER BOOKS

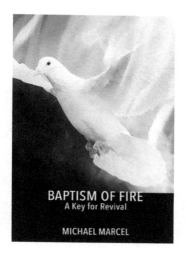

From over twenty years of studying revival history, I believe that a key reason for us not having experienced one in England for over 100 years is the lack of people being Baptised with Fire.

This booklet shows how critical the Baptism of Fire was in past UK revivals. Packed full of testimonies from people who have experienced this wonderful and life changing gift, it will help you seek this for your own life and reach others for Jesus.

Revelation 19:10 "For the testimony of Jesus is the spirit of prophecy." What He did for these people he can do for you and your friends.

This book is available through www.ukwells.org

MICHAEL MARCEL'S OTHER BOOKS

"Michael Marcel has made himself a student of Revival. His thorough approach to any task, coupled with his passion for Jesus, make this a great resource for anyone seeking and praying for revival. Revival remains the cry of my heart, a cry which was ignited in a Pastor's House where every Friday night I attended a prayer meeting for Revival, just after I was saved in 1973. It is stirred again as I read. This book will prompt you to prepare and pray for Revival."

Paul Manwaring
Director Global Legacy & Deployment,
Bethel Church Redding, CA.

This book is available through www.ukwells.org

MICHAEL MARCEL'S OTHER BOOKS

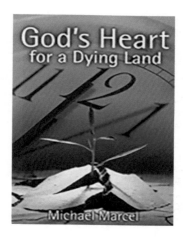

'God's Heart for a Dying Land', is a passionate cry from the heart of one who yearns to see the Church take its rightful position in today's society. It is rich in history and would be an invaluable resource for anyone who has a burden for the nation and who wants to translate that into prayer that brings about lasting change.

Agu Irukwu
Senior Pastor
Jesus House for all Nations (RCCG)

This book is available through www.ukwells.org

MICHAEL MARCEL'S OTHER BOOKS

"In this book Michael raises questions and offers some solutions for the future reformation of the church; including the need for people to turn their faces and gifts towards our society so that it can be changed. You will find this book a worthwhile challenge."

Dr Sharon Stone
Founder and Apostle
Christian International Europe

This book is available through www.ukwells.org

UK WELLS

It is our vision to make available as much information as possible about how and where God has moved across the United Kingdom in the past, so that Christians today will know what happened in any particular area across the nation & then pray again for God to send an awakening for this generation.

Every time we speak or read about our Christian Heritage we are giving testimony to the work of Jesus:

For the testimony of Jesus is the spirit of prophecy.
Revelation 19:10

We have to understand what God has done in the past, so that we can see what He is doing now and understand what He will do in the future.

Our website records thousand of revival report from towns, cities and the countryside across the United Kingdom. You can read the stories of ordinary men and women of God who saw revival break out in their meetings. And there are videos to watch from the locations where God moved about some of the heroes of faith.

Visit, Learn, Pray.

www.ukwells.org

BV - #0033 - 020724 - C0 - 216/138/3 - PB - 9781908154408 - Gloss Lamination